PAPERFOLD WILD ANIMALS

MEGAN MONTAGUE CASH

WORKMAN PUBLISHING, NEW YORK

T0016760

For Winter

Library of Congress Cataloging-in-Publication Data

Names: Cash, Megan Montague, author.
Title: Paperfold wild animals : 10 amazing punch-out-and-fold paper creatures / Megan Montague Cash.
Description: First edition. | New York : Workman Publishing, [2022] | Audience: Ages 7 and up | Identifiers: LCCN 2021043213 | ISBN 9781523512768 (paperback)
Subjects: LCSH: Paper work—Juvenile literature. | Wildlife art—Juvenile literature.
Classification: LCC TT870 .C336 2022 | DDC 745.54--dc23
LC record available at https://lccn.loc.gov/2021043213

Book design by John Passineau and Lourdes Ubidia
Photographs of folded paper models by David Lewis Taylor
Author photo by Jack Dyson
Alamy: Imagebroker p. 16; Nature Picture Library p. 42; WaterFrame p. 24.
Getty Images: David Buzzard - media-centre.ca p. 38; Jim Cumming/Moment p. 8; Morne Green/iStock p. 28; Jurgen & Christine Sohns p. 32; Paul Souders/Stone p. 12; Lillian Tveit/EyeEm p. 36; Stuart Westmorland/Corbis Documentary p. 20.

Workman books are available at special discounts when purchased in bulk for premiums and sales promotions as well as for fundraising or educational use. Special editions or book excerpts can also be created to specification. For details, please contact the Special Sales Director at special.markets@hbgusa.com.

Workman Publishing Co., Inc., a subsidiary of Hachette Book Group, Inc.
1290 Avenue of the Americas
New York, NY 10104
workman.com

Distributed in Europe by Hachette Livre, 58 rue Jean Bleuzen, 92 178 Vanves Cedex, France.

Distributed in the United Kingdom by Hachette Book Group, UK, Carmelite House, 50 Victoria Embankment, London EC4Y 0DZ.

Printed in China on responsibly sourced paper.

First printing March 2023

10 9 8 7 6 5 4 3 2 1

How to Create Paperfold Wild Animals

Learn these **five general skills** for folding the animals. Then refer to individual instruction pages. Note these paper animal crafts are rated from basic to complex. Even the easier ones can require some time and patience, so start small, and ask for help if you need it.

❶ SEPARATE

Tear out a template page from the book. Carefully release perforated animal template from page. (Dispose of any small paper scraps.)

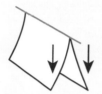

❷ FOLD

Mountain folds, marked with **solid blue lines:** Paper gets folded down; fold line is visible on edge of fold. Most folds are mountain folds.

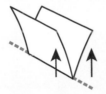

Valley folds, marked with **dashed blue lines:** Paper gets folded up; fold line is hidden inside.

Pleats, which combine both kinds of folds: A dotted area with a dashed line on one side and a solid line on the other indicates a pleat. **Dot patterns** show areas that will be hidden or tucked away when animal is folded.

HOW TO MAKE A PLEAT FOLD

a) Press (fold) tail down at solid mountain lines, so tail goes inward.

b) Lift tail outward, reversing the fold, while pressing in dashed valley lines.

c) Pinch to create neater pleats. Dots will be mostly hidden.

PRO TIPS: Once paper is bent, it can't be unbent. Take your time and be precise. Your animal will thank you!

Folding Technique:
• Fold templates along the blue fold lines.
• Work on a clean, flat surface.
• Press firmly along edges to make crisp, flat creases.

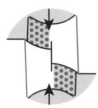

③ JOIN

Interlocking slots connect by lining up slots, then sliding the two tabs together.

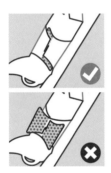

Arrange the tabs so they are tucked *inside* the animal, rather than outside the animal. Dotted areas on tabs will be hidden when this is done correctly.

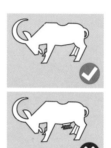

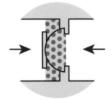

Mushroom tabs + slots connect by inserting tab into corresponding slot. The dotted tab is hidden inside when connected correctly.

④ SHAPE

Some animals require careful **curling** or **bending**.

⑤ COMPLETE

After assembly, compare with photograph. Gently make any adjustments necessary, and make sure all feet rest on surface.

The more you fold, the better you'll get. Become an expert and earn your paper-folding diploma (see page 43)!

Place thumb here for best tear! ➔

Created by Megan Montague Cash

Wolf

Rating:
Basic

INSTRUCTIONS

1 Fold wolf template in half along solid spine line, pressing entire length, including tail, into a crisp, flat crease. Unfold to continue.

2 At base of tail, gently press tail down at solid V-shaped fold lines so tail is pushed inward between legs.

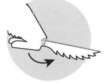

3 Lift tail outward, reversing the fold, while pressing nearby dashed (valley) fold lines in, creating a pleat. (Dotted area should be hidden.)

4 At front legs, fold solid lines. Then interlock leg slots so dotted tabs are tucked inside.

5 Place wolf sitting upright on surface. Tail should sit along surface.

6 Pinch folds at base of tail with thumb and forefinger, matching position in photo.

Wolves

Classification: Mammal

Scientific name: *Canis lupus* and other species

Location: North America, South America, Europe, and Asia

Terrain: Forests, mountains, tundra, deserts, plains, and grassy areas

Climate: From temperate to extreme

Diet: Carnivore

Size: Up to 5.5 feet (1.7 m) long

Weight: Up to 175 pounds (79.4 kg)

Life span: Up to 13 years in the wild

● Wolves are the largest members of the dog family. The modern domestic dog (*C. lupus familiaris*) is not only closely related to wolves, but actually classified as a wolf subspecies.

● Wolves howl to communicate, to establish territory, and as a warning.

● Wolves live and hunt in organized family units called "packs," which usually have from six to ten members.

● In the spring, when there are new puppies, wolves move to a "den," which can be in a cave, a hole they dig, or at the base of a hollow tree.

● A wolf pack may roam large distances on a hunt—up to 12 miles (19 km) in a day.

● Wolves prey mainly on large herbivores (plant eaters), such as deer, elk, moose, caribou, and bison.

● After a hunt, a mother wolf will feed her pups by regurgitating chewed-up food stored in her stomach.

Created by Megan Montague Cash

Bear

Rating:
Basic

BEAR INSTRUCTIONS

1 Fold bear template in half along solid spine line, pressing entire length into a crisp, flat crease. Unfold to continue.

2 At shoulders, fold solid (mountain) fold lines, then fold dashed (valley) fold lines in, creating a pleat. Flatten folds at shoulders.

3 At base of tail, gently press tail down at solid V-shaped fold lines so tail is pushed inward. Then lift tail outward, reversing the fold, while pressing nearby dashed (valley) fold lines in, creating a pleat. Pinch folds at base of tail.

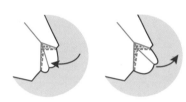

4 At head, create a final pleat, gently pressing the solid (mountain) fold lines and dashed (valley) fold lines. Adjust tilt of head to match photo, and pinch folds at head.

5 At chest, fold solid lines. Then interlock chest slots so dotted tabs are tucked inside.

FISH INSTRUCTIONS

1 Fold fish template in half along solid spine line, pressing into a crisp, flat crease, allowing top fin to remain above fold.

2 On tail fin, very gently interlock tiny tail slots so sides line up with each other.

3 Carefully insert fish into bear's mouth slot to match photo.

Bears

Classification: Mammal

Scientific name: *Ursidae* (family)

Location: North America, South America, Europe, and Asia

Terrain: Forests, mountains, tundra, deserts, and grassy areas

Climate: From temperate to extreme

Diet: Omnivores (eating meat or vegetation); polar bears are carnivores, and pandas are herbivores.

Size: Up to 8 feet (2.4 m) long

Weight: Up to 1,600 pounds (725.7 kg)

Life span: Up to 25 years in the wild

● The largest species of bear is the Arctic polar bear, which can weigh 1,600 pounds (725.7 kg). The smallest is the sun bear of Southeast Asia, which weighs 150 pounds (68 kg) or less.

● A male bear is called a "boar," a female bear is called a "sow," and a baby bear is called a "cub."

● Bears have excellent sight, are highly intelligent, have great memories and navigation skills, and can use tools. (For example, they can use a barnacle-covered rock to scratch an itchy bear face.)

● Bears can smell food, predators, or other bears from up to 20 miles (32 km) away.

● In the winter, most bears don't eat, drink, pee, or poop. They mostly sleep in their den (a hole, cave, hollow tree, or dug-out snow cave). This isn't technically hibernation, which is when an animal's breathing and heart rate slow way down.

● Adult bears generally have few natural predators. Six species of bear are vulnerable, mostly because of human impact on their habitats.

Created by Megan Montague Cash

Place thumb here for best tear! ➡

Ibex

Rating:
Moderate

INSTRUCTIONS

1 Fold ibex template in half along solid spine line, pressing entire length into a crisp, flat crease. Unfold to continue.

2 Between head and shoulders, gently press dashed (valley) fold line into neck while pressing solid V-shaped fold lines on either side. When dotted area is folded into neck, flatten the folds.

3 At head, fold solid lines, then gently cross and interlock head slots. Fold flat into place, taking care not to bend horns.

4 Carefully tuck small tabs into slots on either side of neck. Flatten folds at head, neck, and shoulders.

5 Fold all solid lines at legs.

6 At belly, fold solid lines. Then interlock belly slots so dotted tabs are tucked inside.

7 Gently spread horns and ears apart to match photo.

Ibexes

Classification: Mammal

Scientific name: *Capra*

Location: Europe, Asia, and Africa

Terrain: Chaparrals, forests, and mountains

Climate: From temperate to extreme

Diet: Herbivore

Size: Up to 5.5 feet (1.7 m) long

Weight: Up to 265 pounds (120.2 kg)

Life span: Up to 18 years in the wild

● Ibexes are wild mountain goats and make their home on high, remote cliffs, inaccessible to many predators.

● Ibexes have been spotted as high as 22,000 feet (6,705.6 m) above sea level.

● Ibex hooves are sharp-edged and can expand and contract, with concave bottoms that can grip surfaces like suction cups.

● Ibexes can leap more than 6 feet (1.8 m) straight upward.

● All ibexes have horns. Male ibex horns can reach up to 5 feet (1.5 m) long, with the females' slightly shorter. Only male ibexes have beards.

● A baby ibex is called a "kid." Kids remain with their mother for at least a year.

● Ibexes migrate from lower to upper mountain slopes (and back again) throughout the course of the year.

● Ibexes spend most of their lives eating.

Created by Megan Montague Cash

Place thumb here for best tear! →

Lion

Rating:
Moderate

INSTRUCTIONS

1 Fold body piece in half along solid spine line, making a crisp, flat crease, but stopping at tail. Unfold to continue.

2 At base of tail, gently press tail down at solid V-shaped fold lines so tail is pushed inward near legs, making a valley fold along short dashed line. Allow most of tail to remain flat. Fold solid tail tuft line into a mountain fold. Curl tail upward to match photo.

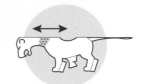

3 At neck/shoulder, gently press down at solid V-shaped fold lines so head is pushed inward between legs. Unfold. Press dashed (valley) fold line in, reversing the fold, lifting head upward, and creating a pleat. When head is set into correct location, pinch folds at neck and shoulder to crease.

4 Fold all solid lines at legs.

5 At belly, fold solid lines. Then interlock belly slots so dotted tabs are tucked inside.

6 On mane piece, fold solid lines crisp and flat, one at a time.

7 Position mane around front of chest. Then pull ears to outside of mane. Carefully tuck long tips of mane into hole in spine. Match mane positioning to photo.

Lions

Classification: Mammal

Scientific name: *Panthera leo*

Location: Southern, Central, and East Africa; India

Terrain: Savannas, grasslands, dense scrub, and open woodlands

Climate: Dry

Diet: Carnivore

Size: Up to 10 feet (3 m) long

Weight: Up to 550 pounds (249.5 kg)

Life span: Up to 16 (female) and 12 (male) years in the wild

● Lions are the second-largest cats in the world (after tigers).

● A group of lions is called a "pride." A typical pride consists of up to three adult males and a dozen adult females, plus cubs. Lionesses are the primary leaders and hunters in the pride.

● Lions mainly hunt and devour large herbivores, including antelopes, gazelles, zebras, hippos, and rhinos.

● Although the lion is often referred to as "the king of the jungle," lions do not actually live in jungles.

● A lion's roar can be heard as far away as 5 miles (8 km).

● The size and color of a male lion's mane determine much of his status in life.

● Lion cubs are born spotted and blind.

● Lions can run up to 50 miles per hour (80.5 kph) and can leap as far as 36 feet (11 m).

● Without their coats and markings, lion and tiger bodies are virtually identical.

Created by Megan Montague Cash

22

Crocodile

Rating:
Complex

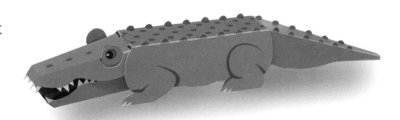

INSTRUCTIONS

1 On both template pieces, fold every fold line (both solid and dashed) into a crisp, flat crease. On body piece, make sure back and tail ridges protrude.

2 On body piece, gently join interlocking slots behind eyeballs.

3 On head piece, gently join interlocking slots behind eyeholes.

4 Insert eyeballs into eyeholes (lowering top of head onto bottom of head).

5 At back of head, insert mushroom tab into slot at neck. Pull mushroom tab gently (from underside) until it's locked into place.

6 At tail, insert mushroom tab into slot and push until it's locked into place. Aligning this may require gentle wiggling.

7 At belly, gently interlock belly slots so dotted tabs are tucked inside.

8 Tail edges should be tucked gently inside back legs, and head should sit inside shoulders, as shown in photo.

9 At front of jaw, carefully line up mouth panels to match photo.

Crocodiles

Classification: Reptile

Scientific name: *Crocodylia*

Location: Africa, Asia, Australia, and the Americas

Terrain: Wetlands

Climate: Tropical

Diet: Carnivore

Size: Up to 20 feet (6.1 m) long

Weight: Up to 2,200 pounds (998 kg)

Life span: Up to 75 years in the wild

● Crocodiles are the world's largest and heaviest reptiles.

● The ancestors of the crocodile shared the world with dinosaurs—they have changed very little in 200 million years.

● To tell a crocodile from an alligator, look at the snout. Alligators have broad, U-shaped snouts, while crocodiles' are longer, tapered, and V-shaped. Alligators are found only in North America and China, while crocodiles are found in many parts of the world.

● A crocodile's jaws can apply 5,000 pounds (2,268 kg) of pressure per square inch.

● Female crocodiles lay eggs on land, about 12 to 48 per nest. Hatchlings are 8 to 12 inches (20 to 30 cm) long at birth and grow about a foot each year until maturity.

● A mother crocodile carries her hatchlings in her mouth.

● Crocodiles make a variety of sounds, including growls, grunts, and hisses.

● Lost crocodile teeth grow back swiftly. A crocodile can go through 8,000 teeth in a lifetime.

Created by Megan Montague Cash

Giraffe

Rating:
Complex

INSTRUCTIONS

1 Fold body piece in half along solid spine line, pressing entire length, including tail, into a crisp, flat crease. Unfold to continue.

2 At base of tail, gently press tail down at solid V-shaped fold lines so tail is pushed inward near legs, turning dashed tail line into a valley fold. Pinch folds at base of tail. Fold solid tail tuft line into a mountain fold. Adjust tail angles to match photo.

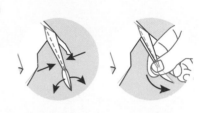

3 Fold all solid lines at legs. At shoulders, gently press dashed (valley) fold line into body while pressing solid V-shaped fold lines on either side (at slots). Flatten folds. Unfold to continue.

4 On either side of chest, gently fold solid lines. Then gently press dashed (valley) lines below chest. (Do not flatten folds.)

5 Fold neck and head template in half along spine line, making a crisp, flat crease. Unfold to continue.

6 Unfold neck and body templates. Position neck above body. Carefully insert mushroom tabs into neck slots, and push gently until both mushroom tabs are locked in. Let dotted neck-support tabs hang down into body.

7 At chest, carefully insert mushroom tab into slot until it's locked into place.

8 At hind legs, interlock leg slots so dotted tabs are tucked inside.

9 At head, gently interlock small slots so sides line up. Spread ears apart slightly to match photo.

Giraffes

Classification: Mammal

Scientific name: *Giraffa camelopardalis*

Location: Southern, Central, and East Africa

Terrain: Savannas, grasslands, and open woodlands

Climate: Dry

Diet: Herbivore

Size: Up to 19 feet (5.8 m) tall

Weight: Up to 4,250 pounds (1,927.8 kg)

Life span: Up to 26 years in the wild

● The giraffe is the world's tallest living mammal. A full-grown giraffe's neck can reach 6 feet (1.8 m) long—yet contains only seven vertebrae (neck bones). There are 33 vertebrae in the human spine.

● A male giraffe is called a "bull." A female is called a "cow." A baby is called a "calf."

● A giraffe's heart is 2 feet (61 cm) long and weighs up to 25 pounds (11.3 kg).

● Giraffes make a variety of low-frequency sounds below the range of human hearing.

● Giraffes eat up to 75 pounds (34 kg) of leaves a day, preferring those of the acacia tree. A giraffe tongue measures up to 21 inches (53.3 cm), making it useful for reaching the highest leaves. Giraffes have stomachs with four compartments and spend most of their lives chewing.

● At 6 feet (1.8 m) high, an adult giraffe's legs are taller than the average adult human. Giraffes eat, drink, sleep, mate, and give birth standing up.

← Place thumb here for best tear!

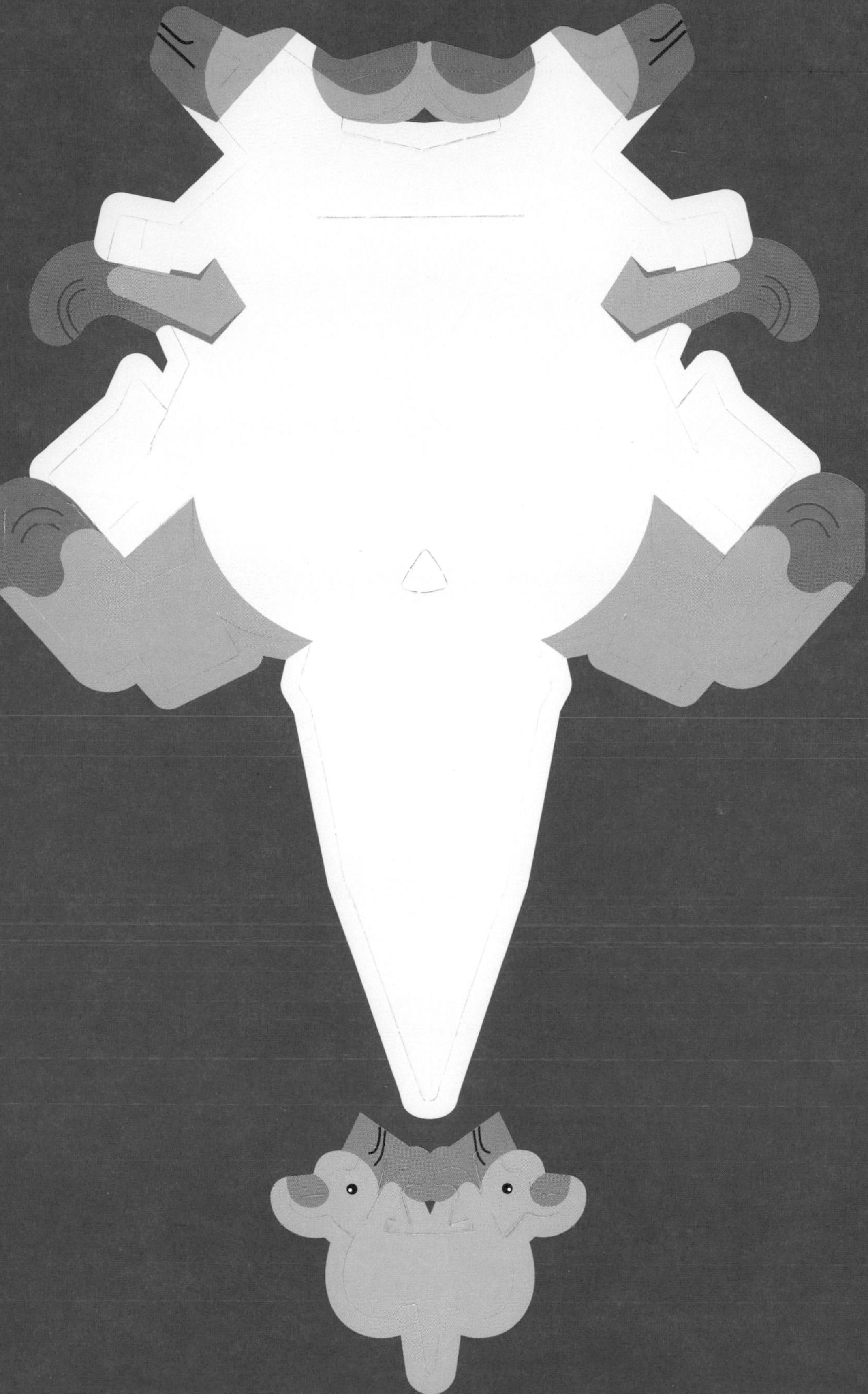

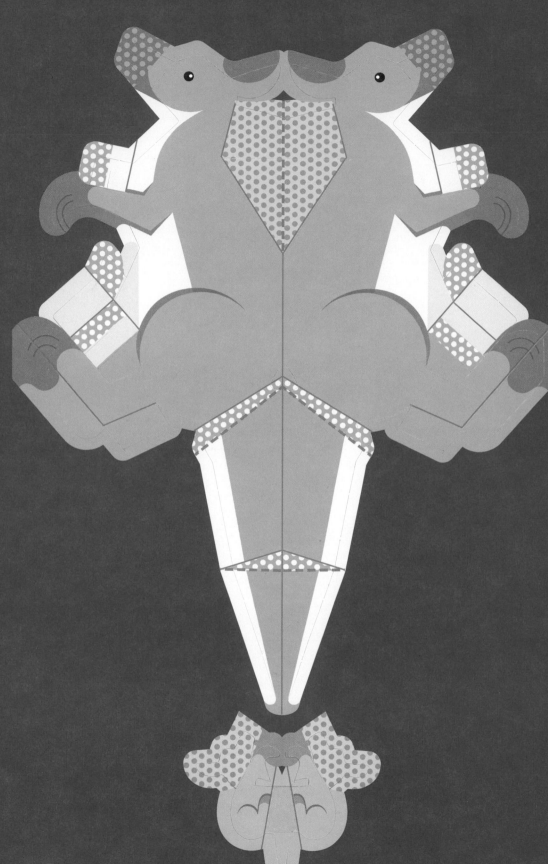

Created by Megan Montague Cash

Kangaroo

Rating:
Moderate

INSTRUCTIONS

1 Fold kangaroo piece in half along solid spine line, pressing entire length, including tail, into a crisp, flat crease. Unfold to continue.

2 Between neck and back, gently fold dashed (valley) fold lines into body while creasing solid fold lines on either side. When dotted areas are folded into body, flatten the folds.

3 At base of tail, gently press tail down at solid fold lines, pushing tail between legs. Then lift tail outward, reversing the fold, while pressing nearby dashed (valley) fold lines in, creating a pleat. Repeat at middle of tail. Pinch all tail folds to crease.

4 Fold remaining solid lines at legs, feet, chest, and multiple pouch tabs. At chest, interlock tiny chest slots so dotted tabs are tucked inside.

5 At head, gently interlock small slots so sides line up.

6 At pouch, carefully interlock slots so dotted areas are hidden. Fold pouch into belly so tabs are tucked on either side of pouch. Spread ears apart slightly to match photo.

JOEY INSTRUCTIONS

1 On baby template, fold solid lines crisp and flat, one at a time. At neck, gently interlock tiny slots so sides line up with each other.

2 Insert baby into mother's pouch, clipping slot behind arms onto (double-thick) pouch front panel.

Kangaroos

Classification: Mammal

Scientific name: *Macropodidae*

Location: Australia, New Guinea, and Bismarck Archipelago

Terrain: Grasslands, deserts

Climate: Dry

Diet: Herbivore

Size: Up to 6 feet, 7 inches (2 m)

Weight: Up to 200 pounds (90.7 kg)

Life span: Up to 6 years in the wild

● Kangaroos are the world's largest marsupial (pouched) mammals.

● A male kangaroo is called a "buck," a "boomer," or a "jack." A female is called a "doe," a "flyer," or a "jill." A baby is called a "joey."

● All female kangaroos have a frontal pouch where their babies eat, sleep, and develop. A joey is ready to leave its mother's pouch for short periods after 4 months and be on its own after 10 months.

● The scientific name for kangaroo means "big foot" in Latin.

● Kangaroos duel, or "box," using their claws and feet as weapons.

● Kangaroos have no kneecaps and can't walk. However, they can hop up to 30 feet (9.1 m) in a single jump.

● When a kangaroo senses danger, it will thump its large tail on the ground to warn the others in its herd.

● Kangaroos are very good swimmers.

● Kangaroos mainly eat grass and small plants. They are hunted and consumed by Indigenous peoples across Australia.

Created by Megan Montague Cash

Orangutan

Rating:
Complex

INSTRUCTIONS

1 On both template pieces, fold every fold line (both solid and dashed) crisp and flat.

2 Place leg template onto body template's corresponding dotted hexagon panel. Blue triangle should meet blue triangle. Legs should tuck under body with bent knees up.

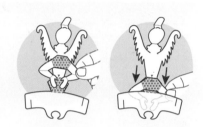

3 Wrap body under arms and around to back, creating a chest cylinder. Then gently interlock back slots so dotted tabs are tucked inside.

4 Orangutan's back should align with its bottom. Adjust if necessary.

5 Hook collar around to back of neck.

6 Fold head into place, and insert chin dotted tab into chest. Adjust legs to match photo.

Orangutans

Classification: Mammal

Scientific name: *Pongo*

Location: Asia (Sumatra and Borneo)

Terrain: Rain forests

Climate: Tropical

Diet: Omnivore

Size: Up to 5 feet (1.5 m) tall

Weight: Up to 300 pounds (136.1 kg)

Life span: Up to 40 years in the wild

● The orangutan is the only great ape native to Asia.

● In the Malay/Indonesian language, *orangutan* means "person of the forest." Orangutans are the world's largest tree-dwelling animals.

● Orangutans communicate with their hands and mouths, use tools, and can understand complex ideas.

● Although orangutans' legs are short, their wingspan can reach up to 8 feet (2.4 m) long.

● Orangutans eat fruit, leaves, and vegetation, and will also eat flowers, bark, insects, eggs, and, on occasion, meat.

● In the wild, adult male orangutans may fully develop cheek pads (known as flanges) by around age 30. Females select mates based in part on the impressiveness of these flanges.

● Female orangutans give birth only once every eight years, the longest period between births in the animal kingdom. A young orangutan spends the first seven years of its life in constant proximity to its mother.

● In the wild, orangutans make a new sleeping platform, or nest, every night.

Elephant

Rating:
Moderate

INSTRUCTIONS

1 Elephant body piece is prefolded along the spine. (Do not separate panels along the spine line!) Fold spine so dotted areas are exposed.

2 At base of tail, gently press tail down at solid V-shaped fold lines so tail is pushed inward between legs, turning dashed tail line into a valley fold. Pinch folds at base of tail. Fold solid tail tuft line into a mountain fold. Adjust tail angles to match photo. Press flat at intersection of tail and tuft.

3 At chest, fold solid lines. Then interlock chest slots so dotted tabs are tucked inside.

4 At belly, fold solid lines. Then interlock belly slots so dotted tabs are tucked inside.

5 Fold head template in half on solid line. Crease, then unfold.

6 Fold solid lines at top of head so dotted triangles are tucked inside.

7 On head, angle upper part of trunk inward, creating pleats on either side. Repeat on lower part of trunk. Curl trunk inward and pinch folds.

8 Connect body and head, carefully inserting each tusk through holes in head. At the same time, tuck dotted triangles into space at neck.

9 Press head gently into body until it fits snugly to match photo.

Elephants

Classification: Mammal

Scientific name: *Elephantidae*

Location: Subtropical regions of Africa and Asia

Terrain: Savannas, grasslands, forests, deserts, swamps, and highlands

Climate: From temperate to extreme

Diet: Herbivore

Size: Up to 13 feet (4 m) tall

Weight: Up to 7 tons (7,000 kg)

Life span: Up to 70 years in the wild

● The elephant is the world's largest living land animal.

● Elephants are extremely intelligent animals with excellent memories.

● A male elephant is called a "bull," a female is called a "cow," and a baby is called a "calf."

● The oldest female in an elephant herd leads the group.

● Mother elephants carry their young for up to 22 months. Newborn calves can weigh more than 200 pounds (90.7 kg).

● An elephant's trunk can weigh up to 290 pounds (131.5 kg), can grow to 7 feet (2.1 m) long, and has about 40,000 muscles. Trunks are used for breathing, smelling, spraying, feeding, feeling, grooming, making noise, moving things, and hugging fellow elephants.

● Elephants don't get much sleep (they're always foraging for food). When they do sleep, they often do it standing up.

● Both male and female African elephants grow tusks, but among Asian elephants, only males have them.

Tortoise

Rating:
Basic

INSTRUCTIONS

1 Fold tortoise template in half along solid spine line, pressing entire length into a crisp, flat crease. Unfold to continue.

2 At front of shell, gently press dashed (valley) fold line into shell while pressing solid V-shaped fold lines on either side. When dotted area is folded into shell, pinch to crease.

3 At back of shell, gently press solid V-shaped fold lines so tail is pushed inward between legs. Then lift tail outward, reversing the fold, while pressing nearby dashed (valley) V-shaped fold lines in, creating a pleat. Pinch folds to crease.

4 At bottom of shell, fold solid lines. Interlock shell slots so dotted tabs are tucked inside.

Tortoises

Classification: Reptile

Scientific name: *Testudinidae*

Location: North America, South America, Europe, Asia, and Africa

Terrain: Deserts, wetlands, tropical forests, and mountainous terrain

Climate: From temperate to extreme

Diet: Herbivore

Size: Up to 6 feet (1.8 m) long

Weight: Up to 575 pounds (260.8 kg)

Life span: Up to 150 years in the wild

● Tortoises are a land-dwelling relative of turtles. They usually have high-domed shells and stubby legs, and most of them are herbivores.

● Turtles and tortoises are ancient species believed to have first appeared around 220 million years ago.

● Tortoises have one of the longest life spans of any animal—80 to 150 years.

● Tortoises have very good memories and can recognize human facial features.

● Tortoises have both an exoskeleton (shell) and an endoskeleton (skull, bones).

● Tortoises don't have teeth, but they do have beaks; they smell with the roofs of their mouths.

● Tortoises travel only up to 0.3 miles (0.5 km) per hour.

● The largest tortoise is the giant Galápagos tortoise (up to 6 feet, or 1.8 m, long), and the smallest is the speckled Cape tortoise (4 to 6 inches, or 10.2 to 15.2 cm).

Paperfold University Diploma

Paperfold University

_____

(your name / your group's name here)

has successfully mastered the five skills of

Separating, Folding, Joining, Shaping, and Completing

and has hereby earned a

PhD (Paperfold Handskills Doctorate)

in **Wild Animal Construction**

and is granted associated

interlocking entitlements and pinching privileges.

Awarded under the seal of this authority on

this _____ day of _____ , _____ .

   (day)   (month)   (year)

Megan Montague Cash PPA

Professor of Paperfold Animals

Paperfold University

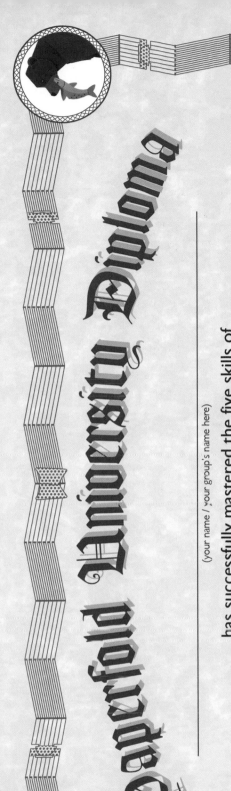

ABOUT THE AUTHOR

Photograph by Jack Dyson

MEGAN MONTAGUE CASH'S favorite things include animals, paper, color, design, and learning. She has been folding paper animals since she can remember and is excited to share this passion with you.

Megan was encouraged by her artist parents to make things with her hands. Today she is an illustrator, author, and designer with a focus on work for children. She has created folded paper projects for Nickelodeon and the Museum of Modern Art. Her books include *What Makes the Seasons?* and the Bow-Wow series. Her work has won numerous awards and has been translated into museum exhibits, curricula, and different languages.

Megan graduated from Pratt Institute in Brooklyn, where she now teaches a specialized course in designing for children.